PETER
THE VEGETARIAN ANTEATER

a vegetarian rhyming story

by Benny Bellamacina
illustrations by G. E. Palmer

NEW PUDDLE PRESS

Mum and Dad Anteater
had many concerns
about their son Peter,
who wouldn't eat worms...

He wouldn't eat bugs
he wouldn't eat spiders
and worst of all,
he announced...

"I'd rather eat my pants
Than eat ants."

"But you're an Anteater"
Quibbled Grandma Rose,
"Why do you think
You've got that big long nose?"

"How disgraceful!
Never in the long line
of bushy-tailed Anteaters
has a family member
refused to eat ANTS!"

Angrily chirped in Great Cousin
Norman, in one of his regular rants...

Peter shrugged his shoulders
and went to his bedroom
to escape all the family
doom and gloom
Then...
the bedroom door shook
with a RAT A TAT TAT!
it was Peter's father...
demanding a chat.

Peter's father,
a rather large anteater
stormed in the room, and
bellowed at Peter,

"I haven't gotten this big
eating carrots, cabbage and tofu!
I eat ants, we all EAT ANTS!
So why can't you?"

The next morning at breakfast there was one empty chair...
They all searched the whole house

Peter just wasn't there.

Great Uncle Ron
looked in the cupboard...

The suitcase with initial the "P"
had gone...

Grandma Rose
followed her very long nose,
down the garden path
but found,
only a rusty old bath

Sister Maria
searched the woods,
but she came back
with only a handful of buds

Great Cousin Norman
jumped in his truck,
driving for miles,
without any luck

Mum and Dad Anteater
hurried and hurried
to catch the bus to town,
they were so so worried.
They searched the shops
the cafe, the Post Office
and the town square
but Peter just
wasn't anywhere...

Then finally,
in the town library,
there was Peter
all alone
reading a book on Rome.

Mum and Dad Anteater gave Peter a big hug. They cuddled him up, and took him home.

Welcoming Peter home,
Uncle Ron
straightened his dickie bow,
scratched his big toe, and said
*"Peter, you're the only
vegetarian, librarian
Anteater I know."*

The whole family laughed
and lived ant-illy ever after.

Copyright © Benny Bellamacina
G.E. Palmer
and the publishers

First published in 2018
by New Puddle Press
the children's imprint
of New River Press

printed by SRP, Devon, England

design and typesetting
by New River Press
ISBN: 978-1-9996310-2-4

NEW PUDDLE PRESS

The author illustrator and publishers retain the copyright, publication and intellectual property rights on the material in this book in accordance with the Copyright Designs and Patents Act 1988